For Dearest Ahsana

Nana & Nani

January 2001

THE STORY OF
MAHABHARATA

Retold by
Bani Roy Chowdhary

HP

Hemkunt Press
A-78, Naraina Indl. Area Phase-1 New Delhi-110028

Fourteenth Revised Edition 1994
Fifteenth Impression 1997
Reprinted 1999
ISBN 81-7010-158-1

Books in this Series

Stories from Panchatantra
More Stories from Panchatantra
Stories from the Arabian Nights
More Stories from the Arabian Nights
Sindbad the Sailor
Aladdin & Alibaba
Fairy Tales from India
Folk Tales from India
More Folk Tales from India
South Indian Folk Tales
Tales from Eastern India
Stories of Birbal and Akbar
Tales of Birbal and Akbar
Aesqp's Fables
Folk Tales from Mauritius
Jatak Tales
The Story of Ramayan
The Story of Mahabharata
The Story of Krishna
The Story of Guru Nanak
Life Story of Guru Gobind Singh
Life Story of Guru Nanak
Story of Mohammad The Prophet
The Story of Buddha
The Prophets of God
Tales from Indian Classics
More Tales from Indian Classics
Tales from Indian Mythology
Story of Hanuman
Story of Maharaja Ranjit Singh

Printed at H.K. Batra & Sons, New Delhi-110028

Contents

The Pandavs and the Kauravs

The Mahabharata is a story about the Pandavs and their cousins the Kauravs, and the great war they fought for the throne of Hastinapur.

When Pandu, the King of Hastinapur, died, his eldest son was very young. So his brother, a blind old man, became the King. The hundred sons of the blind king were known as the Kauravs. Duryodhan and Dusasana were the elder two Kauravs. The sons of Pandu were known as the Pandavs. They were Yudhisthir, Bheem, Arjun, Nakul and Sahadev.

Though the princes grew up together, the Kauravs were jealous of the Pandavs. Duryodhan wanted to be the next king but he knew that Yudhisthir was the rightful heir and would eventually become the king. However, he refused to give up.

One day he said to the blind king, "Father, declare me heir to the throne. The eldest son always succeeds his father. Why shouldn't I ?"

The king sadly shook his head. "No son, that cannot be. I too want you to become the king but Yudhisthir is the heir to the throne. The people also love him because he is kind, brave and truthful. I cannot go against the wishes of the people."

"In that case grant me one wish."

"What is that ?"

"Send the Pandavs away for at least one year," said Duryodhan. "I shall try to win the love of the people."

"And where am I to send them ?"

"Send them to Varnavarta, a beautiful city on the banks of a river."

What was Duryodhan's plan, the king wondered. He did not question him because Duryodhan would not tell him. Instead he sent for the Pandavs and said to them, "You have been in Hastinapur for a long time. Go to Varnavarta with your mother for a change. It is a beautiful city."

The Pandavs looked at one another. Why were they being sent away so suddenly ? They were sure that this was Duryodhan's plan but they did not question it.

The people of Hastinapur bade them a sad farewell.

Soon after they left, Duryodhan called one of his trusted men and said, "Go to Varnavarta immediately and build a beautiful house for the Pandavs. It must be made of lac and other things that burn easily and quickly. Sprinkle perfume everywhere to hide the smell of lac. Paint and decorate the house so that the lac is not visible. Guard the house and when I give orders, set fire to it. And then," said Duryodhan, rubbing his hands gleefully, "my cousins will die and I will become the heir to the throne. But be careful. No one must suspect us".

A large house was built of lac, wax and wood. The walls were brightly painted and beautiful paintings hung on them.

Everything was completed before the Pandavs arrived.

"What a beautiful house," Bheem exclaimed. "Look at those beautiful balconies and arches. The furnishings and paintings in these rooms are better than those we have at Hastinapur."

Suddenly Bheem put up his hand and sniffed the air. He looked around questioningly and sniffed again.

"I smell lac," he whispered.

His brothers sniffed the air and nodded their heads. Bheem was right. There was a strong smell of lac. All the perfumes could not hide the smell.

"We must be careful," whispered Yudhisthir. "I think Duryodhan plans to kill us. I'm sure he will set fire to this house".

The Pandavs began to live in their new house, always watchful. One day their uncle Vidura sent a man.

"I have been sent to dig a tunnel from the house to the banks of the river," the man said. "You must escape by that route if there is any danger.

"What danger does uncle Vidura expect ?" Bheem asked.

"The guard will set fire to the house as soon as he receives orders from Duryodhan. My orders are to start work immediately".

The man wasted no time. He set to work with great speed. He worked only during the night because he did not want the guard to know and thus warn Duryodhan.

In the meantime, the Pandavs hunted and enjoyed themselves.

The guard was happy to inform Duryodhan that the brothers did not suspect any plot. The Pandavs, on the other hand, were happy that the guard did not know about the tunnel.

A year passed. Duryodhan still waited. The Pandavs became more alert than ever. Arjun was getting restless.

"One of these days the guard will receive his orders and set fire to the house," he said. "Before he can do that, let us set fire to it ourselves and escape. That will fool our cousin".

"That is a wise suggestion," mused Bheem."Thinking us dead, Duryodhan will be very happy but just watch his face when he sees us alive."

"We're not going back to Hastinapur," Yudhisthir said.

"Oh" said Bheem and kept quiet. He never questioned his eldest brother.

One dark night the Pandavs set fire to the house and escaped through the tunnel. The house of lac shot up in flames and the sleeping guard died in the fire before he could save himself.

The news spread to Hastinapur and the people were full of grief. But in the palace, the Kauravs were secretly celebrating the death of their cousins. Now , the Kauravs, were the heir to the throne.

It was still dark when the Pandavs came out of the tunnel. They could see their burning house and the flames that lit up the town. People were running about shouting and waving their hands.

The Pandavs walked quickly towards the river. There they found a boat waiting for them.

"Prince Vidura has asked me to row you across to the opposite bank before sunrise," the man said. "No one must know that you have escaped".

"How did uncle Vidura know that we would escape tonight ?" Bheem wanted to know.

"Bheem, get into the boat," Yudhisthir ordered. "There is no time to waste".

They got into the boat and the man rowed them across the river. On the opposite bank was a very thick forest.

The brothers thanked the boatman and quickly disappeared into the thick forest that bordered the river. For the next one year they travelled by night and rested by day to escape the notice of the people.

Marriage of Draupadi

One day Bheem came back very excited. "Arjun, !" he shouted. "Where is Arjun ?"

"What's the matter ?" asked Arjun coming into the room. "I have very good news. King Drupad is holding the *Swayamvar* (when the girl chooses her husband and garlands him) of his daughter Draupadi. There will be a test in archery. The winner will marry the princess . Aren't you going to try your luck ?"

"How can I ? Only invited kings and princes go to a *Swayamvar*".

"But common people also go. And what if none of the kings and princes wins the test ?" Bheem asked.

"In that case, there is a chance. Do you think I should go ?" Arjun asked Yudhisthir.

"Yes, I think you should. You are the best archer and can easily win any test".

"If you win, you become Drupad's son-in-law and Drupad you know, is rich and powerful. He can help us," Bheem said.

"Bheem is right," Yudhisthir said. "We need help to get back our kingdom and only Drupad can help us."

The brothers set out for Panchala, Drupad's capital. It was bursting with activity. News of Draupadi's beauty had spread far and wide. Kings and princes from distant kingdoms had come to try their luck. Duryodhan too was amongst them.

The Pandavs, dressed as poor brahmins, took up quarters in the poorer part of the city. No one recognised them.

On the morning of the *Swayamvar*, all roads led to Drupad's palace. The brothers followed the crowd and sat down with the common folk. By and by the kings and princes came to the glittering court of Drupad and took the seats of honour set apart for them. Drupad sat on his throne. Draupadi with a garland in her hands, sat next to him.

When all were seated, Drupad said, "I have set a test. The man who wins the test, marries my daughter. Near the pool over there you can see an unstrung bow. Directly overhead on the ceiling is a golden fish revolving at high speed. The man who wants to marry my daughter, must first string the bow and then hit the eye of the fish with one arrow. This he must do by looking at its reflection in the water."

The kings and the princes smiled. They were all expert archers or so they thought, however, whilst most of them could not even lift the bow, those who managed to lift and string it, failed to hit the eye of the fish.

What would happen now ? Everyone wondered. Each one of the royal guests had failed. Would the beautiful princess then remain unwed ?

All eyes turned to Drupad. He announced, "Since the kings and princes have failed, I now invite people from the common crowd to try their luck. The person who wins will marry my daughter."

Immediately Arjun got up and walked towards the pool. He was a tall, handsome man. "How can a brahmin be so tall and muscular ?" the people wondered. "Moreover, he walks like a prince. Who is he ?"

Arjun picked up the bow and strung it without difficulty. Then he knelt down in front of the pool, took careful aim and shot an arrow at the fish. It hit the eye. The crowd went mad with excitement. They clapped loudly and cheered Arjun. He hit two more arrows and the fish fell into the pool.

Draupadi got up to garland Arjun. Instantly there was a great commotion. The kings and the princes stood up as one man.

"We will not allow this," they shouted. "No poor brahmin is going to marry the princess".

"Please sit down," begged Drupad. "He has won the test by fair means and shall marry my daughter."

"We will not allow this," they again shouted and drew out their swords. Immediately the brothers joined Arjun, and a terrible fight began. The court was full of fighting men. However, the guests could not match the Pandavs and they retired, furious but defeated.

Draupadi garlanded Arjun. When Drupad learnt that a Pandav had married her, he was extremely happy. He blessed the couple and the two with the other Pandavs returned to their quarters. When they reached home Kunti was inside one of the rooms.

"Mother," they called, "come and see what we have brought with us".

"I'm busy now," she answered from within. "Share whatever you have brought".

"What did you say ?" Yudhisthir asked, shocked.

"I said share whatever you have brought," she repeated. "That's how it has always been."

The brothers looked at one another in dismay. What were they to do ? They had never disobeyed their mother. Could they disobey her now ? Arjun shook his head and this is how Draupadi became the wife of five brothers.

Indraprastha

The Pandavs, now the sons-in-law of Drupad, settled down in peace and comfort. Duryodhan's spies carried every bit of news to him and he did not like what he heard. His plans had once again failed. His cousins were not only alive, they were rich as well.

Karna, his friend, said, "This is the time to attack them. Our army can easily defeat Drupad's."

"That's an excellent idea," agreed Duryodhan.

"Don't be silly," Bheeshma, his grand-uncle said. "Your army cannot defeat the Pandavs."

"The correct thing would be to invite them to Hastinapur and divide the kingdom between the Pandavs and the Kauravs," advised Vidura.

"Impossible," Duryodhan shouted.

"Vidura is correct," his father replied. "I should have divided the kingdom long ago. It's still not too late. I'll do so now. Vidura sent for them immediately."

Within a few days the Pandavs arrived at Hastinapur with their mother. The people had collected outside the city to welcome them. As soon as the chariots were sighted, the people greeted them with shouts of joy.

The brothers went to their blind uncle and touched his feet. He placed his hand on the head of each one of them and blessed them.

"How's your mother ?" he asked.

"She is well," Yudhisthir replied.

His uncle continued, "I have sent for you because I want to divide the kingdom between you and my sons. Hastinapur goes to Duryodhan. You, Yudhisthir, will get Khandavprastha. You will be crowned its king immediately."

Yudhisthir hung down his head and did not speak. He was shocked at this unfair division. Khandavprastha was the rocky, barren part of the kingdom.

Yudhisthir was crowned the king of Khandavprastha. Soon after this, he left for his kingdom with his mother, Draupadi and brothers. Krishna also went with them. He was Kunti's nephew and a close friend of Arjun.

Khandavprastha was indeed a barren land. Rocks and thorny bushes were all over the place.

Arjun was extremely angry.

"What an unjust division," he cried. "I will not let you accept this. What is the use of a desert ? We cannot live here."

"He's right," added Bheem. "Who wants to live here ? Not me."

"I'm the king here," replied Yudhisthir quietly, "and I will stay here."

"But why ? Why should you stay here ?" Bheem wanted to know. "You're the real king of Hastinapur, not Duryodhan."

"That may be true........" Yudhisthir began.

"Not may be, it is true," Bheem corrected him.

"Alright, but uncle has made me king of this kingdom and who are we to judge our elders ?"

"We should question our elders if they are wrong," said Bheem and Arjun together.

"What are you quarrelling about ?" asked Krishna. He had been listening to the brothers. "What does it matter if this is a desert ! We'll work hard and make this the most beautiful kingdom in the world."

"But that's impossible," put in Bheem sullenly. "Flowers don't grow on stones."

"Nothing is impossible, Bheem," Krishna replied. "I will help you with my workers and we will work a miracle here."

"In that case, we will also help, won't we, Arjun ?" Bheem asked.

The work began. The Pandavs and Krishna's workers worked day and night. Little by little, the capital city grew under their eyes. And when it was completed, it was a feast for the eyes.

"It is as beautiful as Indra's city in heaven," Krishna said, "and so we shall name it Indraprastha."

The fame of this city spread far and wide and people flooded to it. Many settled there and Yudhisthir's kingdom grew rich and prosperous.

Duryodhan heard of the fame of Indraprastha and its king and it made him mad with envy. Once, in order to see how true the rumours were, he paid a visit to Indraprastha.

Palatial buildings and colourful gardens dotted either side of the roads. But best of all was the palace of the Pandavs. Sheets of gold, studded with precious stones, covered the walls. The curtains were of glittering brocade. Wherever Duryodhan turned, he saw the wealth of his cousins. The smiling faces of the people, too, told him of their happiness.

His cousins welcomed him. True, they were surprised at his sudden visit.

"I wonder why he has come," whispered Bheem to Arjun.

Yudhisthir's stern look kept the brothers quiet. He said, "Duryodhan, we are very happy to have you here. Stay with us for a few days."

Duryodhan accepted the invitation but nothing in Indraprastha made him happy. The more he saw the wealth of his cousins the more envious he became. The moment he returned to Hastinapur he went straight to his uncle Sakuni and said, "Uncle, all our plans to destroy my cousins failed in the past. Think out a successful plan now. We must destroy them."

"That is difficult, Duryodhan," Sakuni answered. "They are powerful and popular. We cannot destroy them.

"You mean you're afraid of them."

"No, I'm not. I'm not afraid of anybody," replied Sakuni.

"Then think out a plan," insisted Duryodhan.

"There's only one thing I can suggest."

"And that is ?"

"Steal their kingdom from them."

"But that's impossible" shouted Duryodhan.

"Just listen to my plan before you start shouting. Yudhisthir loves the game of dice. That is his one weakness. Invite him here and challenge him to a game."

"But I can't play well. He'll defeat me."

"You need not play" assured Sakuni. "I'll play for you. I have special dices. Yudhisthir cannot win."

"What if he refuses ?"

"He will not refuse. I'll see to that."

"And what will the bet be ?"

"First we'll bet on small things and then in the end, it will be your kingdom against his. The winner will get the other's kingdom."

Duryodhan clapped his hands and gave a loud laugh.

"That's an excellent idea. I'll send a messenger immediately. Are you sure you'll win ? I don't want to lose my kingdom."

"Have no fear. I'm sure of victory. Go and send the messenger."

The Game of Dice

Duryodhan went to his father and said, "Father, invite my cousins here for a few days. They haven't visited us for a long time."

"That's true, son. But why this sudden love for your cousins ? I thought you did not like them."

"That's very true," agreed Duryodhan.

"Then why do you want them here ?"

"I want to play dice and Yudhisthir is a good player. I thought we could play a few games here."

"Your plan sounds innocent, but I'm sure you're plotting something."

"No, no, I'm not conspiring anything." Duryodhan added hurriedly.

A messenger was sent and the Pandavs returned with him. Kunti and Draupadi also came with them.

One day, when they were sitting in the court, Duryodhan said to Yudhisthir, "Cousin, how about a game of dice ?"

"I don't play the game any longer," was the reply.

"Why ?"

"It causes a lot of evil."

"Is that the reason or is Yudhisthir afraid ?" asked Sakuni laughing.

"I am not afraid of anything," Yudhisthir replied. "I told you I have stopped playing the game."

"I think you are lying. You're afraid of losing," Sakuni said.

"I am not afraid and to prove that, I'll play one game and one only. Duryodhan, get your dice. We will play now."

"Then don't play," advised Bheem. "Either play Duryodhan or don't play at all."

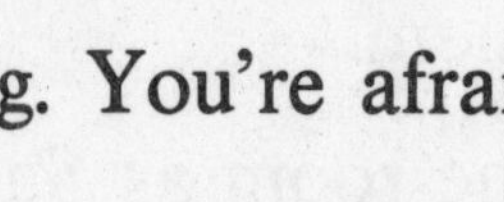

"No, no," Yudhisthir said, "I'll play. I don't care who plays against me. What is the stake to be?"

"My wealth against yours," Duryodhan said quietly.

"Agreed."

The dice rolled and Yudhisthir lost his wealth.

"Play again," he said.

Again and again he played and lost each time; he lost his horses, chariots, servants and soldiers.

"Now what will you bet Yudhisthir?" Sakuni asked with a smile.

"Bet your kingdom against mine," Duryodhan said quietly.

A gasp went around the room.

"But that is ridiculous," shouted Bheem. "You cannot win or lose your kingdom on the turn of a dice."

Duryodhan did not speak. He was looking at Yudhisthir. The eldest Pandav was shocked but Sakuni had made him angry and he was determined to play.

"I accept."

"Brother don't do this," his brothers begged but he refused to listen to them.

A hush fell over the room as Sakuni threw the dice. The dice rolled and with it rolled away Yudhisthir's kingdom.

"I've won" exclaimed Duryodhan. "Now I am king of Hastinapur and of Indraprastha. Cousin, shall we call an end to the game."

"Why should he? He's got his brothers, hasn't he?" mocked Sakuni.

Yudhisthir, ashamed of his losses, lost his senses and bet his brothers one after the other. He lost all of them. They stood there, shocked and silent.

"Now what will you bet ?" laughed Sakuni.

"He doesn't have anything more to bet," jeered Duryodhan. He looked around and a wicked smile lit up his face. "Yes he has and a very precious one," he said.

Everyone looked at him waiting to know as to what he was aiming at.

"He has Draupadi. Yes, cousin, you still have her. Bet her," Duryodhan said and laughed.

"Are you mad Duryodhan ?" Vidura asked. "How dare you bring Draupadi into this ?"

"Uncle, keep out of this. This is between me and my cousin." "How about it, cousin ? Will you bet her or are you afraid to lose her ?"

"I told you I'm not afraid of anything. I'll bet her."

Sakuni threw the dice and Yudhisthir lost Draupadi. The court was as silent as death. Everyone waited for Duryodhan to speak. He sat quietly for a while and then said, "Yudhisthir, I'll give you one more chance. If you win, you will get back your kingdom and everything that you have lost. But if you lose, you will be exiled for twelve years. The thirteenth year you will hide so that no one knows where you are. If you're found during this year you'll be exiled for another twelve years but if you succeed in hiding for that one year, you'll get back your kingdom. Agreed ?" Yudhisthir had no choice.

"Agreed," he said.

But he lost again. Now Duryodhan, the king of two kingdoms, rose and said to one of his brothers, "Take off the rich clothes of the Pandavs. These now belong to me."

The Pandavs removed their clothes and were given some torn rags to wear. But Duryodhan was not satisfied. His success seemed to have gone to his head. He shouted, "Bring Draupadi here. She is now our slave."

"Shame on you, Duryodhan," Bheem shouted "Don't you dare insult Draupadi."

Duryodhan looked sternly at Bheem and said, "Don't forget that you are my slaves now, and slaves don't raise their voice like this." He asked his brother Dusasana to bring Draupadi here."

Dusasana hurried into the palace to obey his brother. He found Draupadi and said to her, "Your husband has lost you in a game of dice. You now belong to Duryodhan. Come with me to the court."

"I don't believe you," said Draupadi.

"You'll believe me when you go to court. Come with me."

"I refuse."

"Don't or I shall drag you there."

"You won't dare," Draupadi said.

"That's what you think. Will you come or will I have to drag you there ?"

"I refuse to go."

Dusasana caught hold of her long hair and dragged her through the palace rooms into the court. The courtiers watched shocked but silent, all except Duryodhan. He shouted, "Dusasana take off her *sari*. It now belongs to us."

"Don't you dare," shouted Bheem.

"Shut up," Duryodhan shouted back. "Dusasana do as I tell you."

Dusasana caught hold of her sari and began to pull. Draupadi fell down and cried, "Help-Krishna help."

"Ha ! ha !" laughed Duryodhan. "Go on, call Krishna. Let's see if he can help you now."

Draupadi continued to chant "Krishna-Krishna."

Suddenly, Duryodhan stopped laughing. The people were all staring at Dusasana. The more he pulled, the longer the *sari* became. Sweat fell from his forehead; the folds of the *sari* made a huge mound and it still grew. At last tired and helpless Dusasana threw away the *sari* he held in his hand and sat down. No one spoke for a few moments. Then Bheem's voice boomed.

"Duryodhan, you have done an evil thing today. I promise that one day I shall kill you and also pluck out Dusasana's right hand."

With these words, the Pandavs took leave of Kunti and left for the forest. Draupadi went with them.

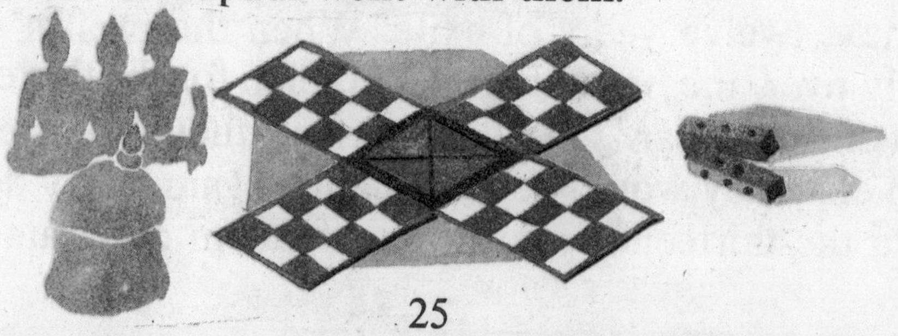

The Exile

The Pandavs and Draupadi faced great hardships during the next twelve years of exile. When the twelfth year was nearly over, the brothers began to plan for the thirteenth and most difficult year. They had to ensure that no one recognised them else they would be exiled once again. They decided to spend the thirteenth year in the kingdom of Virata.

"We will have to, of course, go in disguise," Yudhisthir began. "I think I'll become a minister in the King's court. Bheem, what will you be ?"

"Yes, you're so fat and huge, its easy to recognise you," mused Arjun.

"I'll go as a cook," beamed Bheem. "All cooks are fat. Moreover, I'll be sure of getting enough to eat. These twelve years have nearly starved me."

Everyone laughed. Bheem did not approve of this. He picked on Arjun.

"Arjun, why don't you dress up as a girl. You can dance and sing quite well, can't you ?" He said.

"Do you think I cannot disguise myself as a woman ?" challenged Arjun. "Of course I can. I'm handsome and if I dress with care, I'll make a beautiful woman."

"Of course you will," assured Bheem. "You'll go as a woman to Virata's court. Agreed".

Yudhisthir laughed.

"What's this Arjun ? You're not serious about this, are you ?"

"Of course I am. I'll teach the ladies of the court to sing and dance."

The twins decided to look after the horses and cows of Virata.

"And what will Draupadi do ?" Bheem asked.

"Don't worry about me. I can make lovely garlands and sell them to the queen."

After having decided who will go as what, the Pandavs left for the kingdom of Virata.

When they neared the capital of Virata, they disguised themselves and one by one they entered the service of the king. They passed eleven months without any trouble but in the twelfth month Draupadi was in trouble. The queen's brother fell in love with her. One day he proposed to her.

Draupadi said, "I have five husbands. How can I marry you ?"

"Don't worry about them. I'll kill them. No one is stronger than I am."

"Bheem is stronger than you."

"Bheem ? After thirteen years in the jungle either he's dead or half dead."

No matter what Draupadi said, the man continued to propose to her every day. When Bheem got news of this, he was furious. One night, when he got the chance, he killed him.

The queen's brother had been a friend of Duryodhan. When Duryodhan heard of the manner of his death, he said, "He was a very strong man. Only Bheem could have killed him. This means that Bheem is in Virata's palace. Karna, get the army ready. We'll attack Virata immediately. Thirteen years aren't yet over. If the Pandavs are recognised, they'll have to return to the forest for another twelve years. That will really finish them off."

Duryodhan was pleased. Within a few days, he led his army in to the Virata's kingdom. There was panic in Virata's capital. Virata hurriedly assembled his men and set out to meet the attack.

Bheem was thrilled when he heard of the coming battle. He ran after Virata shouting, "Give me permission to go with you, please."

"But you're only a cook," Virata answered surprised. "My army is made of soldiers not of cooks."

"But I'm not a cook," bewailed Bheem. "I am Bheem. Bheem, Do you understand ?"

"You mean you are Bheem, the Pandav ?"

"Yes," Bheem hurried to answer, much relieved.

"Then come. But wait. Where are your brothers ?"

"There's Yudhisthir," Bheem said pointing to one of the king's ministers.

"Where ?"

"I am here," Yudhisthir replied coming to them.

"What, You're Yudhisthir," exclaimed Virata.

"Surprises ! Surprises !"

"More to come," beamed Bheem. "But let's make a start."

"What about your brothers ?" Virata asked again.

"Don't worry about them. They'll come. Wait till you see who Arjun is," chuckled Bheem.

Riding in front of the army they went out to meet the army of Duryodhan. Suddenly Virata reined his chariot.

"Who's that ?" he screamed. "How is that woman riding a chariot."

A woman was riding a chariot. But even as they looked, the long hair fell off. She also removed her jewels and to the astonishment of Virata, he saw a man stand up.

"But, but" he stammered. "That was a woman. Now I see a man."

"That's Arjun," beamed Bheem.

"Arjun ? You mean to say that Arjun had passed off as a dancing girl for one year ?"

Virata, by now thoroughly confused, rushed into battle. On the opposite side, Drona, Duryodhan and Karna were leading the army. Drona was the first to recognise Arjun and he was happy to see his favourite pupil again. Duryodhan too recognised him and he happily exclaimed, "The Pandavs will have to return to the jungle for another twelve years."

"Why ?" Drona asked.

"Because they've been recognised and thirteen years aren't over as yet."

"I'm afraid you're wrong Duryodhan," answered Drona. "The thirteen years were over a few days ago."

Duryodhan was terribly angry and upset.

"Karna, give orders to attack immediately," he thundered.

The fight was fierce but Virata's army was too good for Duryodhan's. The Kaurav's army was beaten back and it retreated in great haste.

Back in Virata's palace, the Pandavs were in high spirits.

"How I enjoyed beating back Duryodhan's army," Arjun said.

"How they fled when we chased them," chuckled Bheem.

"That's all very good," Yudhisthir replied, worried.

"We have made Duryodhan very angry. I wonder if he'll agree to return Indraprastha to us."

"Stay with me while you send a messenger to him," Virata said. The Pandavs agreed. They sent a messenger to Hastinapur, asking Duryodhan to return them their kingdom. He refused.

"Tell your masters," he said to the messengers, "That I refused to return Indraprastha. If they want it, they'll have to fight for it."

The Battle

Preparations of the war began. Arjun said, "I'll go to Krishna and ask him to join us. If he's on our side, we will definitely win."

"That's right," agreed Yudhisthir. "Start immediately. There is no time to lose."

Arjun set off. When he reached Dwarka he found Duryodhan already there. The palace-guard was sent in to inform Krishna of their arrival. He returned saying, "Krishna is asleep. Please come in and wait."

The men escorted him into Krishna's room. Krishna was lying asleep on his sandalwood bed. A beautiful throne stood at the head of his bed; a cloth of gold was spread out near his feet. Duryodhan without much ado went straight to the throne and sat down. Arjun sat down at Krishna's feet. They waited in silence. After some time Krishna moved and got up, rubbing his eyes. When he opened them, he saw Arjun. He heard Duryodhan's voice and turned around.

Duryodhan said, "Krishna, I arrived first so I should get first preference. I want your help in the coming war."

"True, you came first but I saw Arjun first," Krishna replied. "So I'll be fair to both. I offer my whole army to one. I shall be a charioteer to the other because I've made up my mind not to fight in this war. Duryodhan, since you came first, you can make the first choice.

"I'll take your army," Duryodhan replied without a moment's hesitation.

Duryodhan returned, a happy man. Krishna's army was made up of some of the best soldiers. Moreover, if Krishna did not fight, what was the use of having him ?

Arjun, on the other hand, was happy to have Krishna on his side, even if only as a charioteer.

Having assembled their men, the two armies marched to

the battlefield of Kurukshetra.

On the morning of the battle, the armies stood facing each other. Krishna was Arjun's charioteer. When Arjun saw Drona, his cousins, grand-uncles and uncles on the other side, he said, "Krishna, what is the use of this war ? We are going to fight our own people. We may kill them. Isn't that a sin ?"

"No, it isn't," Krishna replied. "Your cousins are unjust. They have taken away your kingdom and you must fight them."

"But what is the use of the kingdom if one has to kill one's own people to get it ? I don't want the kingdom. I'm going back."

"What ? And give up the war ?"

"Yes. I don't want to kill my own people."

"Arjun, I didn't expect you to speak like this. Always remember that you will have to fight for truth and justice. Even if your own people are on the other side, you must still fight. It is not whom you fight that is important but what you fight for," Krishna said. He explained many things–right and wrong, life and death and so on. All these are to be found in the sacred book of the Hindus, the Bhagvad Gita.

The war began. The armies of the Pandavs and the Kauravs consisted of thousands of men, horses and elephants. They clashed and fought in full fury. The morning sky was covered with clouds of dust. Elephants trumpeted and horses neighed in terror as swords flashed all around them. Men were killed in large numbers on both sides. Before the day was over,

the battlefield was covered with corpses. With sunset, the conch was sounded and the armies withdrew to their camps.

The terrible battle between the cousins went on day after day. Thousands of men and animals died each day, but neither side could defeat the other. Duryodhan was furious and anxious too. No matter how well his men fought they could not defeat the Pandavs.

In the Pandav camp, the brothers too were worried. If the war went on like this, men and animals would die in countless numbers unnecessarily.

One day after Arjun had gone off to another part of the battlefield. Yudhisthir called Abhimanyu, Arjun's son, and said, "Drona has today arranged his army in the form of a wheel. Only Arjun knows how to break this formation. Has he taught you how this is done. ?"

"Yes, he has but not how to get out."

"Don't worry about that," Yudhisthir answered. "You lead, we'll follow close behind."

Abhimanyu felt proud to be entrusted with this task. He was only sixteen years old but he was as brave as his father. He jumped into his chariot and whipped his horses. The chariot shot over the bumpy ground and before the Kaurav army could stop him, he had broken the formation and entered the enemy lines. The Pandavs were close behind but the moment they made an attempt to enter the enemy camp, Jaydrath, one of Duryodhan's generals, stopped them. He and his men put up a stiff fight. The Pandavs fought fiercely because they wanted to reach their nephew.

"Bheem, somehow we must get in," Yudhisthir urged. "Abhimanyu is alone. Duryodhan's men will surely kill him."

"We cannot fight these men without Arjun's help."

"But we don't even know in which part of the field he is. If we stay here, we'll get killed," said Sahadev, the youngest twin.

"But Abhimanyu ? What is going to happen to him ?"

Bheem did not answer. He turned back and rode away. The twin stayed with Yudhisthir for a while longer but they too could not match the strength of Jaydrath and his men and they rode back, taking Yudhisthir with them.

Abhimanyu looked back. His uncles were nowhere to be seen. What had happened ? He wondered. The Kaurav warriors crowded around him. Fearless and determined to fight to the last he took up his bow. Then the fight between the young boy on one side and great warriors on the Kaurav side began. Arrows rained on him but he fought on. Drona and

Duryodhan were watching the fight. After some time Drona said, "That boy is too good for our men. They cannot defeat him."

"Then what should we do ?"

"Karna, you, I and our four great warriors will have to attack him in a planned way," was Drona's answer.

"What do you mean, 'a planned way' ?" Duryodhan asked.

"Each man will have to attack different parts of the boy's body. That is the only way to kill him."

Duryodhan called the other five warriors and they stood in a ring around Abhimanyu. The boy's body was covered with wounds and blood. His eyes were dull with pain. He watched the seven famous Kaurav warriors crowding around him and knew that his end was near. But he fearlessly faced the men. They attacked him as already planned. Abhimanyu fought back but the game was over. The plan of Drona worked. One arrow struck his heart and he fell down dead.

A cry of victory rented the air.

"This will teach the Pandavs a lesson," Duryodhan said. "They may now give up the war."

"Don't fool yourself, Duryodhan," Drona said. "The Pandavs will not give up the war."

"What about Arjun ? His son is dead."

"That may make him determined to kill us, the seven men who killed his son."

"You never say a word of encouragement, do you ?" Duryodhan said and walked away without waiting for a reply.

Arjun's Revenge

The news of Abhimanyu's death was carried to the four Pandavs. They broke into tears. Yudhisthir was full of remorse.

"I have killed the boy," he cried. "I sent him to his death. What will I tell Arjun ? How will I tell him that I killed his son ?"

"Don't talk like that," Bheem consoled. "It wasn't your fault."

"Of course it was my fault. I forced him to go to the front even when he had said that he did not know how to get out."

The brothers returned to their camps sad and heart-broken. With sunset the armies too returned to their respective camps. No fires were lit in the Pandav camps. All the men were in tears. There was silence and darkness all around.

Arjun, returning with Krishna, noticed this and said, "Krishna, I wonder what has happened. Our camp is so silent and dark."

"Let us hurry and find out."

The two men saw the tearful faces of the soldiers and became all the more curious. When they saw the four Pandavs in tears, Arjun and Krishna looked at each other. Then Krishna asked, "What is the matter, Yudhisthir ? Why is every one in tears ?"

Arjun looked around.

"Where is Abhimanyu ?" he asked. "Everyone else is present. Where is my son ?"

"Arjun I have killed your son," wept Yudhisthir. "I've killed Abhimanyu."

"What do you mean ?"

Yudhisthir related the day's happenings. Arjun did not weep; he did not shout. He became angry—angry not with his brother but with Duryodhan and his warriors who had so cruely killed him. But most of all he was angry with Jaydrath.

"He is the man to blame," he said. "If he hadn't stopped you, my Abhimanyu would still be alive. I'm going to kill him first."

"That's impossible," Bheem hastened to say. "He defeated all four of us."

"That may be, but I'm going to kill that man tomorrow before sunset or I will kill myself."

With these words he twanged his bow and Krishna blew his conch. The brothers were happy. They knew Arjun would keep his vow.

The Kauravs, on the other hand, were celebrating the death of the boy. They were sure that the Pandavs would retire to the forest and give up all thoughts of war. Suddenly they heard the twang of Arjun's bow and the sound of Krishna's conch.

"What does it mean," Duryodhan asked. "I thought Abhimanyu's death would cause fear and panic in the camp."

"Didn't I tell you that his son's death would only make Arjun more furious ?" said Drona. "Let us see what our spies have to report."

The spies reported Arjun's vow. The news made Duryodhan very angry. He was also a little worried because he knew his cousin always kept his vows.

He called a meeting of his warriors and said, "We must

protect Jaydrath tomorrow. If we succeed, Arjun will have to kill himself. That will surely be the end of Pandavs."

"Duryodhan, don't entertain false hopes," Drona warned. "There is no one in your army who can defeat or kill Arjun."

"But we can all fight him together and kill him as we killed his son."

"We could do that only because Arjun wasn't there. Do you think Jaydrath could have defeated the Pandavs if Arjun had been present ? Why do you fool yourself and try to fool others and have false hopes."

"You never have anything encouraging to say, do you ?" spoke Duryodhan, red with anger.

"How can I, when I know that we are fighting a losing battle ? You cannot defeat the Pandavs."

"Why then do you stay with me ? Why don't you go over to the side of the Pandavs ?" was Duryodhan's question.

"I am your commander-in-chief and I won't let you down even though I know we will be defeated."

Duryodhan was too angry to speak. He got up and walked away.

The next morning Jaydrath went to Duryodhan and said, "I don't want Arjun to kill me. I'm returning to my kingdom."

"Don't be afraid Jaydrath. My best warriors will guard you," Duryodhan assured. "Arjun will have to fight through three formations before he can reach you. Moreover, Drona will guard the entrance to the first formation.

It was the fourteenth day of the war. There was great excitement in both the camps. Would or would not Arjun keep his vow ?

The sun rose and the war started. The Pandavs were in a killing mood and they killed right and left as they drove through the enemy. Arjun drove to the first formation. Drona was guarding it. Krishna turned the horses away.

"Why are you going away without fighting me ?" Drona asked.

"You are my tutor," Arjun answered. "I cannot fight you. Wish me well."

Krishna skillfully drove the chariot through the first formation but when they came to the second, they met Duryodhan. He put up a fierce fight. By now it was noon and Jaydrath was far away. Arjun was getting worried. He aimed all his arrows at different parts of Duryodhan's body. The Kaurav, badly wounded, fled from there.

Evening was setting in. Arjun had yet to break into the third formation. The warriors of Duryodhan blocked his way and challenged him. Arjun faced them, one by one, and defeated all of them. Then he sped on towards Jaydrath. The warriors guarding him fought Arjun for a long time. Impatient and worried, Arjun succeeded in defeating them. He now faced Jaydrath. The two fought, raining arrows on each other but they fought like equals. It was now nearly evening. Duryodhan looked up hopefully."

"Look," he said to Karna pointing at the reddening sky. "It's nearly time to call a halt to the day's fight. I am sure Arjun will not be able to kill Jaydrath today."

Suddenly the sky grew dark. A cry went up from the Kaurav soldiers, "Jaydrath is saved ! Arjun has failed to keep his vow."

Krishna whispered to Arjun, "Evening has not set in yet. Kill Jaydrath."

At that moment, Jaydrath had put down his bow and was looking hopefully at the dark sky. Arjun wasted no time. His arrow sliced off Jaydrath's head. Immediately the darkness faded away and the setting sun once more shed its feeble light on the battlefield. Arjun twanged his bow and Krishna blew his conch. The entire field knew that Arjun had killed Jaydrath.

Death of Duryodhan

Duryodhan was full of grief. He had lost his best warriors and there was no one to replace them.

"Now the end of the Kauravs is near," he thought grimly. "It is too late to repent now."

Duryodhan was also severely wounded. He wanted to get away from the battlefield. He left it and after walking some distance, came to a lake. The cool waters looked inviting and he dived into it. He hoped the cool waters would cool his body. He stood in the water, only his head above it.

In the battlefield, the Pandavs wondered where Duryodhan had disappeared.

"Where could he have gone ?" Yudhisthir asked.

"I think I saw him walking away from the battlefield," Bheem replied.

"Did he return to his camp ?"

"No, he went that way."

"You mean to say he has left the battlefield and his men ?"

"I think so. Let's go and find out."

So the brothers followed the path taken by Duryodhan and came to the lake. They spotted Duryodhan in the water.

"Duryodhan, why have you come away from the battlefield ?" Yudhisthir asked.

"Don't tell us you have fled in fear," taunted Bheem.

The words stung Duryodhan. He said, "I have not fled. I have lost my friends and relatives in this war. I don't want to live any more."

"But what about your kingdom ?" asked Bheem. "Do you want to give it up ?"

"I don't care for it any more."

"The words sound strange, coming from you," Yudhisthir

said, “Isn’t it rather late to say such things ? It was you who wanted war. Then why flee now ?”

Duryodhan became angry. He came out of the water and picked up his club.

“I will fight you, one by one, to show that I am not a coward,” he shouted.

“I’ll fight first,” Bheem said, coming forward. “Remember the vow I had taken thirteen years ago in your court ? I have to fulfil that vow.”

“You seem very sure,” sneered Duryodhan. “Let’s began.”

Their clubs clashed in mid-air and the fight began. Both were well matched and they fought for a long time. The brothers and Krishna watched.

Krishna whispered to Arjun, "It is only a matter of time."

"What do you mean ?" Arjun asked in a whisper.

"Duryodhan is tired in mind and body. He doesn't have the strength to fight."

At one point, Duryodhan raised his club high and jumped up to bring it crashing down on Bheem's head. Bheem, too, had raised his club and struck. The club hit Duryodhan on his thigh. The bone cracked and he fell on the ground, bleeding.

Bheem was full of joy; he had fulfilled his vow ! But he was still angry with Duryodhan. He raised his foot to stamp the head of his dying cousin but Yudhisthir pulled him away.

"Are you mad ?" he said to Bheem. "It was a fair fight and you defeated him. He is dying. Why then do you want to enhance his agony ? Why must you be unnecessarily cruel ?"

The dying Duryodhan was still hissing with fury and hate.

"You have won this war by unfair means," he accused. "If there had been fair play, you all would be dead."

"If there had been fair play, this war wouldn't have been fought at all," Yudhisthir reminded him.

Duryodhan turned his face away. The Pandavs left him and returned to the battlefield. Duryodhan lay there, dying and utterly alone.

The war was over. The Pandavs drove to Hastinapur in resplendent chariots. The people came out to welcome their new king, Yudhisthir, as he drove into the city.

The brothers entered the great palace where they had

spent their boyhood and lost their kingdom in a game of dice. Krishna led Yudhisthir to the ancient throne of his fore-fathers. There, amidst the chanting of the Vedas and the singing of hymns, Yudhisthir was crowned the king.